Conte

Brol

Imagine

Tell Them

Children's Fears

A Raven's Caw

Outside the Box

To My Darling Heart

Down the Rabbit Hole

The One Who is No Longer Here

Say

Mistakes

How Time Flies By

Never Ending Sleep

Preacher

Escape from Reality

Phoenix

Jealousy

Underwater

The Fruitless Tree

City Life

The End

Goblins in My Head

Definition of Normality

Lady of the Universe

The Lines

Hall of Illusions

You

Lost Cause

Viper's Game

Blue State

Acknowledgements

To put this simply, I would like to thank all my friends and family that have encouraged and supported me during the time I have spent putting together this anthology.

I would like to also thank four particular friends who helped me look over and edit the poems as well as two other friends who helped me design the front cover – I am forever grateful to you all.

Most importantly, I would like to thank God for helping me make this long-time dream of mine become a reality. This book is for you all, as well as for all those who like me, aspires to inspire.

Staring at a Concrete Mirror

A Poetic Take Off

By

Writerlike.k

Broken

Broken...that is how they left me.
They did not even bother mending my damaged joints or attending to the crying of my wounds. The painted features on my face were scratched off and lightly distinguishable, but they did not care; they were not hasty in their actions. My limbs popped out of their sockets then twisted violently, like as if they were trying to form letters with them. The warmth that gave my character a soul was completely flushed out of me, making my wooden, dusty vessel cold and weak. Bits of my ears, nose, fingers, and toes were chipped or rotting away; but they just replied with muffled laughs like they were drunkards, not even remembering the chain of carnage tests they put me through. The fine threads that pulled me off the ground in times of tumult were cut, instantly crippling me for life, but my carers did not care since they were the ones who cut them.
Termites sped up my descent as they began munching down upon what was left of me in their filthy rabbles, cruelly taking advantage of my disabled state. Seeing that I was too damaged, they flung my body off the craftsman's favourite shelf, and into the tin coffin, like a bad, embarrassing memory being thrown into the subconscious of the mind.

I was now trapped...weeping in silence as I watched them close the lid down with a menacing ringing sound, knowing this was the end. Slowly sinking into black, sticky madness, I knew that the soul they made me was now dying out, like a light bulb losing energy to project solid strikes of light against the advancing darkness.
This is how they left me...
Broken.

Imagine

Imagine, imagine this.

Imagine a world that does not rely on besmirched necessities, but rather on pure things, sorting out their priorities as they put first bliss, love and peace. No more pointless insults and disses, no more all-out fights in the streets, no more people cruising with straps and blades, but instead have them standing in unity as they make their hearts emotionally rich.

Imagine, imagine this.

Imagine a world where poverty is nothing more than a faltering myth, promising undernourished orphans, neglected tramps and forgotten widows, that there is more to life than this.
Let us imagine a world where diseases and illnesses are nothing more than empty theories - childish stories that are simply put in place to control the minds of many.
Let us fight them off, train ourselves to annihilate them with powerful punches and deadly kicks.

Imagine, imagine this.

Don't give up now because you're already halfway there, dress your faith in armour and live like as if your biological clocks don't need to tick.

Come, let's imagine.
Let us all stand together...
and start imagining this.

Tell Them

Truth often reveals a warped fidelity to a twisted fact or reality, often showing up the dark secrets of a corrupted government or a brainwashed society.

But in my case, you see, it is a completely different story, for you know that although you have made me into the best man that I could possibly be, I'm just an ordinary guy who will pass away eventually. Which is why, my love, I will leave it to you to pass on memories about me, to tell others of all the notorious aspects and things about me, and how I lived my life fighting off negativity as I embraced positivity. And do not forget to tell them how I will move on from this life as an original because everyone knows that there is only one true me.

So tell them how I relieved myself of all the stains on my soul and sins of my heart, screaming out in the open to the almighty heavens and wishing stars.

Tell them how I learnt that life is not about thug styles and possessions of knives and guns, and tell them how it takes a real man to abide by the law and that crime is anything but fun.

Tell them how much I apologised to you for all the mistakes I made and all the stupid things I had done, and please tell them, how if it was not for you, I would not have been able to complete life's perilous path.

Tell them, tell them how much I loved you and all the things we did as one, and tell them how I was the only man who could acknowledge just how astonishing and striking you really are.

Yes let them hear how I was anxious when exposing my feelings to you at first, but like a bee, your pollen satisfied my thirst.

Tell them…tell them…tell them how although I am gone the beat you started off in my heart has only just begun.

Yes, tell them how my love for you, will never be done.

Children's Fears

They say that the world is your oyster and that you can become anything you want to be, but realistically, that idea becomes a far-off vision or a taunting memory, when you grow up to be an older. Which is why many children create an isolating oasis for their minds to escape to, as they run away from the bad things they do not understand, similar to Peter Pan's Neverland and Alice's Wonderland, they want to rid their eyes of the evil imagery that makes them break out in tears and start going mad as they fool themselves saying how they are never going to grow up and that as long as they are in their own world, nothing can make them blue and sad.

But you can't blame them like they know any better.
For they fear the monsters that prey on them, seeing that their failures make them rejuvenated and happier for they know that they are an easy target, and so play their cards of skullduggery properly so they can capture and trap them under the stained magnificence that keeps them in a horrid order. And because of this, they crave for liberation, for they fear all the trials and tribulations that await them, fearing the day when they become tangled in a web of mortification that eventually leads to their unwanted fruitions.

They dream of an end to their fears, a day when they will not have to wake up to the hisses and growls of their looming peers.
But I say to them to be enduring a little longer, for the journey after this does get better.
But until then, wait patiently and see...
The day when your fears are overthrown, and no longer rule your realities.

A Raven's Caw

Never judge a raven's caw, for we do not know for certain what motivates its eerie call. Settled deep within the shadows of nature, it dares not enter the day's luminous eyes, for it knows for sure, that the moment it steps out into the bright open, its presence will attract nothing but glares and scolds, forcing it to shuffle back into the dark then break down and cry. It yearns for acceptance, grieves for acknowledgement, and prays for more endurance, for its smile has become nothing more than a mask that conceals its sadness. As unpleasant as its caw may be, the raven simply calls out for a friendly deed, for it has had enough of dwelling within a depressing cycle of negativity. It wants to be heard and it wants to be seen, it wants to be referred to great wholesome things that smell nice and are clean, not to the works of a scavenger that taunts from above and feasts upon those decaying away in deep sleep.

Yes like you and me, it simply wishes to break loose, to escape, to be free. So do not ever sway to the darkness that you may feel has cornered you, but be happy and rejoice like never before, for when you next hear...
a raven's caw.

Outside the Box

A young boy comes home from school with bruises black and blue, clearly explaining what sort of mood he is in and why tonight he will not be eating his food, for he will be curled up in the corner of his room, and in the darkness he will pray for a light that can reveal a path that will lead to a life that is clearly the better way, but he knows until such a vision takes place...he will be spending his days in a black and blue cocoon.

You see his peers sneer at him every time he puts his hand up in class and gives the teacher a perplexing yet interesting answer, wishing him to simply wither up and quietly die just like a bee that loses its stinger. But this is not his fault, for he is a simply a dreamer, a developing creator, a thinker, who thinks outside the box.
But what exactly does that mean to think outside the box?

To question the most rudimentary regulations that subtlety holds the minds of many down?

To go on a wild treasure hunt to find rare unusually formed keys that open up to new extraordinary and beautiful worlds that obliviously wait to be unlocked?

Or even to walk amongst a society of wolves when one is clearly a sheep, but would prefer to be different and wear a firm serious face rather than an upside down frown and look like the rest, blissfully ignorant, like stupid clowns?

You see when this young boy grows up to be a university professor, a beloved actor, or even a famous inventor, his peers will be in a trance of bewilderment, questioning when or where or how, did this apparent freak of nature make it in life, while they carry out the nightmarish dead-end jobs that just about help them to pay off their debts and put strain on their shoulders, causing them to become tugged by the strings of uncontrolled drinking and tedious smoking.

For they mistreated his beautiful mind out of immaturity, which is why every time he sees his pasty and drained peers, all looking at him shocked, he would simply say.
"Should've kept your circles out of squares, and thought outside the box."

To My Darling Heart

This is something that I give to you, something unique, something unspeakable, something deep, something that others may register, as something taboo. They can hate and glare, for they don't have a clue, but that does not matter, for the only person who is meant to understand this is you.
Now as I concoct what can only be described as a spotless mirror of my feelings for you, I sit back in my cocoon of relief, for I know for certain, that there is no wrong you can do.

You see, I will paint your personality of pearls on walls, scribble it on floors, fly it through the sky so the world can envision you in awe. I will even brag about it out loud till love itself cannot take any more. For you accomplish beauty ever so simply, making it look easy, your presence alone is a lamp that can light up a bleak room of misery.
So let this be, something enjoyable to see, something to read that can transform your face into an epitome of glee.
Yes, I write this with all the love that I can pluck up, for you are no doubt my darling heart, and if there's one thing I will always regret… is not finding you from the start.

Down the Rabbit Hole

Off I go, down the rabbit hole.
Do not dare get in my way, for the beginning of my journey is now on a roll. You will probably categorise me as crazy, but that is not the case, for my degree of normality basically differs from yours.
You see my mind has had enough of swimming in such boredom waters, waters that will eventually drag me down into a murky abyss of deep blue depression. For others, such an end is acceptable and unavoidable, but for me, it is unacceptable, disgraceful, an unsuitable ending to my life's parable. And my heart, well, let us just say that this choice of mine has made my heart and mind compatible, for it to wants to make my life's tapestry pleasantly describable.
So off I go, down the rabbit hole.
This is my prime objective, my number one goal.
I crave to experience and discover what is not generic to most minds, exploring the unknown wonders of this world, for you see this thought alone throws my bodily senses into a hyperactive alteration for I am excited to see what this adventure can help me dig up and find.
But I know all of this is nothing more than a marred dream to you, so I simply wish all you all the best, right until the day you finally want to know, how to escape this tedious reality, and follow me….
follow me down, the rabbit hole.

The One Who is No Longer Here

A moment in time that seems to horrifically last forever.
A moment in time when happiness becomes devoured as sorrow starts to cruelly take over.
A moment in time where frustrated questions that are soaked in bitter tears are neglected, never receiving their rightful answers.

Now that you are gone the days have seemed to have lost their glow, shimmering weakly as the hours go by tauntingly slow.
Former normal routines become altered by a gothic metamorphosis as your family feel that without your radiance their spirits are dull.
Your friends reminisce about you in a painful silence, yearning for your guidance, craving for your once warm presence, for their bodies have become cold and still, but their minds are lashing out as they want to go down a dark path of provoked violence that will only increase their level of depressed madness.
For you were not a bad person, you just simply like many of us carried deep scars, but it was your way, your style of secreting them from the world, the persona you gave them that led you astray, resulting in you becoming badgered by your poorly selected choice of environment to attire in the title of a fallen star. It is a shame you're gone, for your departure was so sudden, unexpected, unfortunate, for you have become a classic example of time's unpredictable nature, reminding us that it does not wait for us, it only tells us when it gives up on us, when it feels let down by us for not using it wisely the way it taught us, seeing us nothing more as students of failure.
Yes, your departure has made my mind unclear with a curious arrangement of fear, for I too wonder when my time runs out and I have had my moment in the sun, solemnly reminding me of that grim day when I will become the one, who is no longer here…

Say

They say that you are a peculiar annoyance, like an unwanted weed amongst cultivated flowers, but I say your personality is a pleasant memory that will be remembered forever, like an elegant butterfly amongst swollen caterpillars.

They say that your voice is a curse to the ears, but I say it's a musical blessing, a song of healing that can revive those lowly in spirits for your words enlighten even the darkest moments, even when everything seems hopeless and depressing.
They say that you are one of the ugly stepsisters, but I say that your Cinderella, a tiny beautiful gem that is almost hidden by a field of rocky lumps, for when we are together I am often found at the end of jealousy that slithers from other fellas.
They say that we will not make it in life, but I say that we will prosper, for we have each other and all that matters, yes you are my priority, my treasured trophy, that reassuring sign that makes everything better.

They say…they say.
They say that I will never love you and that I will be the enemy who will have you all strung up and hung, but I say…
That I will be your shelter from raging storms because my love for you…has only just begun its run.

Mistakes

See one thing I have learnt in life, is that we all make mistakes, some even though higher on the severity level than others, highlight the limitations we carry as we try to move on and honestly put them down to a formulaic form of human error. Senseless they may be and as harmless as they may seem, mistakes become unerasable scribbles on our lives that spontaneously appear as they slowly try to feed off our subconscious gleam like some sort of parasitic irritancy. And unfortunately, with embarrassment they can make us quake and with guilt they can make us look at ourselves with hate, for we eagerly avoid accepting responsibility for them as we start to view them as a torture stake we must solemnly take, rubbing up against our already scarred shoulders, reminding us of our current unfortunate state.

Yes, we all make mistakes.
Which is why all we can do is hope that they do not resurface and force us to sway to the side effects of sin that forever tries to make our road to recovery anything but straight.
So please, please forgive me when my mind tinkers with my heart which makes my motives falter, for we all now and then stumble and snatch up life's taunting bait.
Because at the end of the day…
We all make mistakes.

How Time Flies By

It is amazing how quickly time flies by.
One minute we are born into a mysterious place we call home, and then the next we have reached an extremely advanced state where we begin to slowly crumble and sadly, die.

Nobody knows how or why time flies by so quickly, for all they believe in is that you only live once and that time is emotionless and impatient, unforgiving to those who mistreat it ever so mindlessly.

It is amazing how quickly time flies by.
Like hunters we try and shoot at its wings to throw it off balance and slow down its speedy flight in order to gain a moment of escapism from a reality of surreal morbidity that it has locked us in, but really, all we are doing is purposely blinding ourselves for time's speed only increases, never decreasing, pilfering our days in this life while our minds wander off into temporary oblivion.

It is really extraordinary isn't it, how quickly time flies by.
Almighty empires have occurred and left the earth like shadows coming and going in the day, the Babylonians, the Persians, the Greeks, the Romans, the Byzantines, even the Ottomans, all now as myths and legends that subconsciously tinker with the way we think and what we say. And with the greatest achievements have also come to the greatest atrocities, from the Higgs boson discovery, domesticating fire, and travelling to the moon, but on the other scale, there's the atom bomb, the holocaust, and the slave trade, all in which linger within the heart of today's modernised society.

Its mind boggling isn't it, just how quickly time flies by.
You see the tracks that time leaves behind is like a portfolio, a room of mirrors that each portray a different part of our lives, from our first day at school, our first time riding a bike, to our prom dance, our first wild holiday, and even our first loves, all in which are unforgettable scenarios.

Yes, it is truly remarkable, just how quickly...
time flies by.

Never Ending Sleep

What is it like, to never wake up?
To forever wander around in a soundless dome that is both lifeless yet bustling with an eerie buzz?
A place where the mind has no matter to overcome and where there is no sense of direction, no down…and no up?
Would you not feel tired, exhausted, frustrated, fed up?

You see my eyes have been sealed shut, but yet they have streams of untamable tears that discreetly seep.
My mouth is trying to construct words, but all the letters are rejected and end up in an evolving heap.
My ears have become numb, but seem to be only functioning when the footsteps of cruel silence slowly creep.
My heart has the urge to dance to an emotional rhapsody, but it is lamenting in its stationary state for the hooks that hold it down run horrifically deep.

So what's it is like, to never wake up?
To be oblivious to life's ongoing bleep and to possess feelings that your heart and soul are forbidden to keep because the things you have sworn to keep outside have now come inside for a peep, stressing that the mistakes you have sown you now must reap.
Yes, I wonder what it would be like, to be trapped, to be in nonexistence, to be in something as grim and bleak…
as a neverending sleep.

Preacher

Preacher, Preacher! Help me Preacher help me!
What is it, dear child? To yell out so loud it must be something dire, something devouring your mind and sapping your sanity, so please come, sit with me and tell me, was is it that has made you holler at me drastically?
Dear Preacher tell me, what am I to do? My conscious is heavy with cysts of guiltiness and I don't know who I can unburden my woes too! My soul is suffocating in its own despair in which it keeps bottled up with the addictive help of alcohol and drugs, but I can no longer take it anymore which is why I've come to you.
Oh dear child, what has become of you? You are like sheep without a shepherd, abandoned, left without a clue. For you among many were deceived into believing that the grass was greener on the other side when really there was no grass on the other side to gaze at in the first place, waking you up to the fact that your hopes and dreams of a better life have been ruthlessly falsified.
Please, Preacher! What must a man that's been indulged in the sinful scale of life since birth do in order to find inner peace, a place of comfort where my mind can unwind and serenely reside?
Ah, my dear child, for this you must exercise faith in our heavenly father and turn to his word and learn his ways, learn how to, despite living in an ungodly world, rely on him and to him pray, pray for a better life and that his hope for the future may arrive soon and forever stay.
But Preacher, what is this hope that you say God has installed for his loyal ones who'll witness such a glorious day?
What hope do you say? It is a hope that was made possible through Jesus' death, history's ultimate sacrifice, in which mankind's slate has been made clean, for God has promised a life without pain and suffering, without fear and death, a time when this poisoned world will be excised...
and replaced with a beautiful paradise.

Escape from Reality

It is a risk I am willing to take.
In order for my mind to undergo some sort of sensation of liberation...yes, it is most definitely a risk I am willing to take, even if it makes my soul quiver and my sanity quake.
I will do whatever it takes.

You see I need a timeout, a refreshing break, for what you call a wonderful world I call a global asylum, and what you see as an advanced society I simply picture as a civilization of fakes. For fatigue is the only thing my body seems to feel, and my ears are swollen from hearing so much nonsense, and with the sheer quantities of tears that have occurred, my eyes have begun to ache.
So now I am fed up, fed up of being surrounded by those who base their morals and decisions on pathetic partialities.
I am fed up with watching people present insanity as normality and normality as something that is nothing more than a preposterous theory.
I am fed up with hearing people speak so arrogantly, acting like their gifts of humanity when really their whole character is anything from human but rather something shockingly beastly.
So like I said, it is a risk that I am willing to take.
But it is worth it, so if you don't mind, I will be leaving on a journey, and making my escape...my escape from reality.

Phoenix

With each fall, I rise.
From the burnt soil I dragged myself out from, I was quickly welcomed, welcomed into an uncompromising world that homed those who only knew how to brutalise, not knowing anything of peace and compassion but only how to be ruthless and uncivilised. They encouraged the defiant flames that scarred my surroundings, rapidly encircling me with intimidating connotations that caused my lamenting options of escape to start misting.

But then I saw it, soaring high in the bleeding sky, a glimmering hope who was like me damaged but ablaze with the tenacity to try.
It reminded me of the imperfection that ran deep through the roots of creation but reassured me that with each tribulation there's a solution.

So as if it were a man, it descended with me, both us painfully bonding with the enclosing field of ashes. But it made me rise, almightily ascending to reach my goal, to claim my rightfully earned prize, making the former oppressors that I surpassed realise that even though like a man I will fall, like the Phoenix…
I will always rise.

Jealousy

Jealousy is a parasite.

Unexpected and almost undetectable when it first encounters its host it slyly carries out its poisonous transformation while remaining hidden out of sight.
For it discolours the soul with a horrendous green, making good things difficult to see as it slowly blurs the line between wrong and right.

Jealousy is a parasite.

It does not care who it strikes, for it simply needs a vessel in order to survive, a hive for it to hide, so it can manifest and ebb out, latching its pincers onto its victim's mind and start injecting them with thoughts of twisted desires and severe strife.

You see, jealousy is a parasite.

It is a fool's sense of ambition.
It is evil's answer to a deadly equation.
It is mankind's kryptonite.

Underwater

I am underwater.
Ascending is simply a fool's vision of hope, for I am descending, being sucked down to a disturbing level where things become unclear and bleaker.
My body seems to be weighed down by an unfamiliar form of depression, and as my eyes feebly gaze up at a blurred surface, that once warm radiance gets weaker and weaker, colder...and colder.
So now I am paranoid, unsure of how many bubbles that are departing from me are left, for their numbers are fiercely diminishing, and the shadows I used to eagerly avoid, are now my new companions on this solemn trip to this murky monotonous void.
My eyes are deliriously ruminating over memories above the surface, above level zero, about a world that was hard but brighter, tough, but better.
But what does that all now matter, for that is in the past, and the reality is, is that I am being brought down to the future which consists of me being silent, anonymous...
Underwater.

The Fruitless Tree

Did I ever tell you about the time I saw the Fruitless Tree? Standing isolated before me, she sheepishly gazed at the cracked earth that homed her decaying roots, with her hunched over body resembling a frown of desertion and misery.
She did not once look up to the emptiness of the sky or at my curious wondering eyes, for heavy hardships weighed down her scarred branches, causing her crown to wither and her once natural glow to reside.

For you see she could not produce any fruitage, which cut her deeply, drove her to a place of insanity, but it was not her fault, she was just born with a disadvantage. But it was due to this that she was viewed by nature as a coarse curse, an unpleasant liability, for if the earth was a song, she would not even be a part of a verse.
For all she's ever wanted is to bear fruit, at least just one, but this a deluded dream, for the despondency that festoons her life clearly highlights that this, can never be done.
So she remains still and upset, subconsciously pondering in an agonising serenity if they will ever be a day when she will bear fruit… And no longer be seen, as the Fruitless Tree.

City Life

Living the city life.

Day by day, night by night, the clocks are constantly ticking on by, restlessly keeping us on the ball as they remind us of the tedious routines that seem to be the foundations of our generic lives: Wake up, time for school, off to work, come home, letters, bills, taxes, families, friends…bedtime.

Living the city life.

From breath-taking monuments to bright flashy lights, ecstatic loud buskers to big fancy shops that buzz with clusters of tourists like irritable flies. Constantly on the go, no time to stop, move and chop move and chop, putting us all on the same ironic wavelength, from those at the bottom right up to those at the very top.

Living the city life.

Walking in the ends, a photomontage of uneven black and grey buildings that are gritty on the outside and even grittier on the inside, along with snaking worn out streets that are badgered by police sirens and music of gangsters. It's nothing but a constant look over your shoulder, for its where ignorant youngers mimic their poor mannered fathers, sadly often finding themselves either in a barred box or in front of a news reporter's camera, either as the victim, or the perpetrator. It's a place where women find it easier to pair up shoes with their makeup than babies with their fathers, and a place where the distinction between man and beast is faulty, for the way they act is unnaturally ghastly, making God wonder if we're any better than the monsters in fairy tales, the creatures we describe as deadly predators.

Living the city life.

So much diversity in ethnicities and nationalities, so much raw talents and arts, so much to discuss and so much to discover in this hectic life of ours, it's just a matter of knowing where to start for possibilities here are so rife, you've just got to go head first on this wild ride.
Yes, this is what it's like…living the city life.

The End

If I told you that it was the end, what would you do?
Would you be rendered speechless, left without a clue?
Would you start to untwist the minds of familiar faces and try to find out just how they really perceived you?

You see if I told you that it was the end, would you feel your sanity starting to become misshapen and bend because the dreams you wished to achieve have now been overthrown by your nightmares, making you quake and wonder whether this is a situation that you can mend?

For you see because of this, hordes of questions begin to make you anxious, so you try bringing the deep things back to the surface, hoping that these things will be the answers you desire, no longer making your mind restless.

You see if it was the end, I'd be seeking out people and trying to make amends, reminisce and sowing up open wounds with them as if it were the latest and coolest trend.
Yes, if it was the end, I'd do my utmost, just for one last time, to love and care, for my family…and friends.

Goblins in My Head

There are goblins in my head, keeping me on my toes, looking out for me as they tell me where to tread, softly, steadily, tread.
If it weren't for them I probably would have ended up in a mad repetitive loop, or even worse, DEAD! But you see no one seems to understand this, for most people cringe at the idea, viewing the goblins in my head as a mental anathema to fear, so they start pouncing to conclusions with scolds as they start to hiss.
I guess ignorance can truly and cruelly be bliss.

You see there are goblins in my head, hums and whispers, using hushed words to paint me pictures, and silent connotations to reassure me that they are honest friends and good listeners, for I feel like most of the time my words are sadly misinterpreted, making me feel down rather than uplifted, which only nudges me closer and closer to a side that's a lot wilder than the side I'm usually on, a side that's undisciplined with a compacted form of crazier.

You see, the goblins in my head evenly weigh out the things in my brain, advising me to keep moving even when I'm drained, and to be prepared for lonely times that'll drench me in its overwhelming rain. But yet people tell me that they are things to dread, that they are the reason why my persona has taken blows and that my sanity has bled, and that they make things worse and far from blessed.

But why?
Is it jealousy, fear of what they can't understand and fear of being misled?
Because as far as I'm aware, the only time I feel a sense of liberation and something more than just a dot to death's grim bed…is when I'm far away from people, and I got the goblins in my head.

Definition of Normality

Define normality for me.
Like honestly, no need for a dragged out explanation of complexity, just simply define this popular word for me.
Because due to our imperfections, we as humans are walking abnormalities, trying to overthrow and dominate one another with flawed theories and contradicting democracies.
So who is in the position to define normality for me?
Because just like one person's beauty is another's ugly, so one person's normality is another's deeply rooted insanity.
You see the point I'm trying to make basically is that our bodies are too stained with irritable idiosyncrasies for us to give life to such a word, for if we did it'd be blatant hypocrisy.
So now seriously, tell me, put my frustrated mind at ease and tell me, what is the definition of normality?

Lady of the Universe

You are a grandiose creature made up of a vortex of love stories gathered from all sorts of awe-inspiring fantasies.
With a quick snap of elegance, you hush swirling galaxies.
With a twirl of your body, you can summon and conjure up all of the planets' energies.
Stars envy your nerve massaging melodies while the moon hides away from your evening rhapsodies that enlighten the looming dusk ever so brightly.
Your beauty even turns the sun onto itself with a disorderly collage of fiery anger.
Yes, you are an intergalactic wonder.
You are…the lady of the universe.

The Lines

The lines between things,

Help me identify what is real and what is an abomination, tearing off duped masks and revealing true characteristics and intentions.

The lines between things,

Help me become more attentive to what is wrong and do what is right by helping me categorise acts of blatant horrific sins and acts that make us luminous with a peaceful and godly light.

The lines between things,

Help me make sure that I do not morph into a beast and remain a man because lately there seem to be more and more excuses to carve images with claws and to reason with roars, so I simply try to stay humane as much as I can.

The lines between things,

Help me stay alive and keep me away from death, exposing this life's deadly snares and enhancing my appreciation for every taken breath.

The lines between things are my saviours, my healers, my teachers, mentors. And even though they don't always run parallel with me, they are the very things that'll make me last forever.

Hall of Illusions

In this hall of illusions, shadows shone like stars while the scattered congregation of weak lights lay in grief and confusion, for it was as if the world had become nothing more than a messy ball of solids and liquids that waited for a proper and guided fusion, someone, or something that could combine and connect it's misshapen pieces and save it from being dragged into a ditch of desertion and depression.

Yes, in this hall of illusions, where echoes of my footsteps became songs of consternation, I saw you smirking beautifully at me, for you brought and told me about this place in rhymes of equivocation. But it had soon become clear that you were going to be the cause of both my survival and fruition, which was all going to take place, in this hall of illusions.

You

You.
You are.
You are the indescribable desire that melts the hearts of those who gaze upon you with a captivating fire.
You are the unexpected hunch that guides me with faint loving voices and sketchy yet reassuring depictions of hope when it comes to the unavoidable crunch.
You are the representation of a perfected completion that is faultless, possessing no deforming defaults or monstrous malfunctions.
You are, the key clue to a life that is entombed by joyous expressions and free of solemn mews so please do not change for anyone because although they may be appearing to support you, deep down inside they are trying to pollute your life with green bubble-like-boos.
So please stay the same, because...
You are.
You.

Lost Cause

The clues you gave me had meaning but were subliminal, for you kept your own agendas hidden within the shadowy limbos of people's minds, making me appear as some sort of psychotic criminal.

And you see it's funny, because I use to brag to my friends and family about how you were my accurate reflection and that you're what I would be if I ever reached an unquestionable condition of perfection, but I guess what I had imagined was nothing more than an immature illusion.

So tell me, where do we go from here?
Because the obvious signs have now been made unclear and while you have moved on with a stainless and uncorrupted slate, I'm left with an unidentifiable state for I have reached a paradoxical peak where joy is something wrong to have and to love is really to hate.
I'm bathing in ambiguousness, for the place I once had has now been taken away and replaced with a place that is roofless and has no laws. I might as well be living in Monstro's jaws because I feel like…
I have become a lost cause.

Viper's Game

Nothing would have stopped me from wanting to be with you despite there being a few unresolved issues.
Problems. Problems that formed heinous hives suspended from the branches of our relationship. They were bearable to overlook at first but had now become the reason we couldn't move on and continue on a path where we both had the same thing to pursue, which was a love lit life that consisted of two simple yet significant pieces, one being me, and the other being you.
So tell me then, why would you choose me to be a contender in this sanity perverting game? Because I know for sure that you did not pick me at random, that much is easy to fathom.

And like every existing thing in this world made up of atoms you made up my heartless downfall, ruining me and haunting my life like as if it was an opera, with you playing the masked phantom.
But you did not care, and I am sure in your deranged emotionless eyes that what you did to me may have seemed pretty fair, supposedly harmless, after all, to you it is just a game, where the objective is simply to ruin as many lives as you can without taking the blame for failure in doing this would be an unfortunate shame, well, at least to you anyway.

You said that I was your number one, or that is what you at least had claimed.
You said that it was always going to me and you, but then reality hit. So instead of feeling some sort of relief, all those words did were plant mayhem in my mind, resulting in my soul going insane and my heart becoming maimed.
You said to me that everything was going to be alright, but I know you only said those words to chain me up with a false hope which kept me unnaturally tamed.
If I only had figured out your fork-tongued words sooner I would not have been played and suffered as one of your futile pawns, leaving

me lost and torn.

For each lie and deceptive act had hooked on me and then cut me over and over as if I was wrapped in a blanket of thorns.

Yes, you are a devious sugar-coated spawn, but hey, I just hope the next guy you meet does not fall for your serpent-like ways, and saves himself from being scarred by shame, and stays far away, from your little game…

The viper's game.

Blue State

I have reached a state that is bluer than your average blues.
I pray that this sort of thing never reaches you, for this is the sort of blue that bruises essences and drowns hearts, but it especially strangles the mind in an inhumane choke that can only be avoided by the very few.

It is a type of blue that comes with great misinterpretation as it often blows things immensely out of proportion, for it puts you in a world where circles are squares and squares are triangles, and lines themselves are broken and bent by breath-stealing distortion.
It is a type of blue, that is often perceived as an insane incoherence, for it only happens to rare people on rare occasions and defies the logic of science so those who become ensnared by this condition of blues often become impaled with sadness, isolating themselves, for their cries are muted and their will to live starts to deteriorate in silence.

Yes, I sincerely pray that you do not experience what I am going through...
A sinister state...that is bluer than your average blues.